T0332148

Who Was
Jesse Owens?

Who Was
Jesse Owens?

by James Buckley Jr.

illustrated by Gregory Copeland

Penguin Workshop

For Robin Soria,
who lives with a couple of heroes of his own—JB

To Jerry, for whom I'm grateful—GC

PENGUIN WORKSHOP
An Imprint of Penguin Random House LLC, New York

Text copyright © 2015 by James Buckley Jr.
Illustrations copyright © 2015 by Penguin Random House LLC. All rights reserved.
Published by Penguin Workshop, an imprint of Penguin Random House LLC, New York.
PENGUIN and PENGUIN WORKSHOP are trademarks of Penguin Books Ltd.
WHO HQ & Design is a registered trademark of Penguin Random House LLC.
Printed in the USA.

Visit us online at www.penguinrandomhouse.com.

Library of Congress Control Number: 2015947741

ISBN 9780448483078   15 14

Contents

CONTENTS

Who Was
Jesse Owens?

In rural Alabama, Jesse Owens sprinted across farmland and ran along dirt roads. He ran to the fields where he picked one hundred pounds of cotton a day. He ran to the orchards where he and his large family picked fruit from the trees. He ran with friends, playing games when they were not working alongside their parents.

Jesse ran because it made him feel free.

"I always loved running," he later said. "It was something you could do by yourself and under your own power. You could go in any direction, fast or slow as you wanted, fighting the wind if you felt like it, seeking out new sights just on the strength of your feet."

"Jesse would run and play just like everyone else," his cousin Mattie Taylor said of those days of playing in Alabama. "But you could never catch him."

No one ever did catch Jesse Owens. The young man who began running barefoot in those Alabama fields became one of the greatest sprinters in history. At the 1936 Olympic Games, he won four gold medals and became an international hero.

Jesse Owens started running when he was just a young boy, and he never stopped.

Chapter 1
Home in Alabama

Henry and Emma Owens were both the children of enslaved people who had lived in Alabama. By the time Henry and Emma married in 1896, slavery had ended, and African Americans were free throughout the United States. But life had not changed much for many Black people.

After Henry and Emma married, they lived and worked on a large farm in rural Oakville, Alabama.

They did not own the farm. They were sharecroppers. That meant that they rented a small part of a larger farm from the owner. When the crops—mainly corn and cotton—were harvested, they received a share of the money from their sale. However, the farm's owner kept money for the Owenses' rent and for some of their food. After all that, the Owens family had very little money left.

Life was very difficult. Throughout the South, laws prevented Black people from being treated equally and having all the opportunities that white people did. These laws were called "Jim Crow" laws.

Henry and Emma had twelve children, three of whom died at birth. Three daughters—Ida, Josephine, and Lillie—survived. They were followed by six sons—Prentice, Johnson, Henry, Ernest, Quincy, and Sylvester.

JIM CROW LAWS

AFTER THE SOUTHERN STATES LOST THE CIVIL WAR IN 1865, WHITE PEOPLE CONTINUED TO DISCRIMINATE AGAINST BLACK PEOPLE, WHO WERE NOW FREE. SOUTHERN STATES PASSED LAWS THAT KEPT BLACK PEOPLE APART FROM WHITE PEOPLE. THERE WERE HUNDREDS OF THESE LAWS. TOGETHER, THEY WERE KNOWN AS JIM CROW LAWS, NAMED AFTER A CHARACTER IN A STAGE SHOW.

BLACK AND WHITE CHILDREN COULD NOT GO TO SCHOOL TOGETHER. BLACK PEOPLE COULD NOT EAT AT WHITE-OWNED HOTELS OR RESTAURANTS, OR EVEN USE PUBLIC SWIMMING POOLS. BUSES AND RAILROADS HAD SEPARATE SEATING AREAS FOR BLACK PEOPLE AND WHITE PEOPLE. THERE WERE EVEN SEPARATE DRINKING FOUNTAINS FOR BLACK AND WHITE PEOPLE.

SOME EIGHTY YEARS LATER, IN THE 1960S, THE CIVIL RIGHTS MOVEMENT PUT AN END TO THESE LAWS.

The entire family lived in a three-room wooden house. It was not well made, and wind blew between the wall boards. The children crowded into two rooms to sleep. There were not enough beds, so some slept on the floor.

In 1913, another son, James Cleveland Owens, was born. Known to everyone as J. C., the boy was the thirteenth and youngest child in the large Owens family.

He suffered from several childhood illnesses. Nearly every winter, he had pneumonia, a dangerous disease in which his lungs filled with fluid. He caught cold after cold and often had bad coughs. He suffered from painful growths on his skin. There was no doctor or nurse nearby, nor any money to travel to visit one.

J. C. grew up working with his family on their farm. There was no school for sharecroppers' children in Oakville. Work came first. When the work was done, one of the adults might gather the children and teach lessons. Food was never fancy—beans and fruit and biscuits made up most meals. The family had meat only on special holidays, such as Christmas and Easter. J. C. later said, "I remember there was no money to buy clothing. I was embarrassed when I saw the neighbor girls and I didn't have enough clothing to fully cover my body."

J. C. knew his life was hard. But he once said, "We had a lot of fun. We always ate."

Together, the Owens family walked nine miles each way every Sunday to Oakville Missionary Baptist Church. During their walks, the family talked of their dreams and hopes. J. C. said that one day he was going to college. No Owens family member had ever gone to college. Such a thing seemed impossible for someone from a poor Black family in Alabama.

Chapter 2
Heading North

Cotton had long been the South's most important crop. In the 1910s, swarms of insects called boll weevils destroyed many acres of cotton. Farmers and sharecroppers like the Owens family suffered, with no crops to sell. At this time, factories were booming in the northern states. Hundreds of thousands of Black Americans moved north to find work in these factories. Many moved to big cities in the midwestern states of Ohio, Illinois, and Michigan.

J. C.'s older sister Lillie was among those who headed north. After settling with cousins in Cleveland, Ohio, she wrote to her mother about the jobs there. As life got harder and harder in Alabama, Emma Owens convinced her husband that the family should try a new life. In 1922, Henry moved with his two oldest sons to join Lillie.

THE GREAT MIGRATION

AT THE START OF THE TWENTIETH CENTURY, NINE OUT OF TEN AFRICAN AMERICANS LIVED IN SOUTHERN STATES. BY THE MIDDLE OF THE CENTURY, THE PROPORTION WAS DOWN TO LESS THAN ONE IN FIVE. THE GREAT MIGRATION LASTED FROM ABOUT 1910 UNTIL THE 1960S. MORE THAN SIX MILLION BLACK PEOPLE LEFT THE SOUTH FOR THE NORTH AND WEST. THEY WERE IN SEARCH OF BETTER JOBS AND BETTER LIVES.

Great Migrat[ion]
1915-1940s

Second Migr[ation]
1940s-1960s

IN NORTHERN CITIES, THE NEW ARRIVALS LIVED IN NEIGHBORHOODS WITH OTHER BLACK PEOPLE. IN SOME OF THESE CITIES, MORE THAN HALF THE RESIDENTS WERE AFRICAN AMERICAN. BLACK PEOPLE FILLED ASSEMBLY-LINE JOBS IN FACTORIES THAT MADE CARS, TRUCKS, AND STEEL.

MANY WOMEN FOUND WORK AS MAIDS OR COOKS
IN THE HOUSES OF WHITE PEOPLE WHO COULD
AFFORD TO HIRE THEM.

THE GREAT MIGRATION CREATED NEW
OPPORTUNITIES FOR MILLIONS OF FAMILIES.

A few months later, he sent for the rest of his family. Before Emma left, she sold nearly all their possessions to help pay for the trip. The sale brought in only $24 (about $300 today).

Things were very different in Cleveland for the Owens family. In Alabama everyone they knew were Black. Now their neighbors included many white people. These people were immigrants looking for a better life just like the Owens family.

In Cleveland, J. C. went to school for the first time. At Bolton Elementary he was put in the first grade, though he was nearly ten years old.

He soon improved his reading enough to move up a grade. When he moved to Cleveland, he was still called J. C. by family and friends. However, his teacher at Bolton misheard his name. She thought it was *Jesse*. The new kid in class, young J. C. was too shy to correct her. From then on, he was called *Jesse* by almost everyone.

The family lived in a large rented house. Henry worked at a steel mill. Emma cleaned houses. All the older children worked as much as they could.

By 1928, Jesse had improved enough academically to attend Fairmount Junior High. He spent hours after school helping out at Tony's Shoe Repair. He also worked at a greenhouse and made deliveries for a grocery store.

The money helped the family buy food and clothes and pay the rent.

While he was in junior high, Jesse met Minnie Ruth Solomon. She was a friend of his sisters. Soon they were dating. "I fell in love with her the first time we ever talked," he later said. Known as Ruth, she was also from the South, having grown up in Georgia. They would be together for the rest of Jesse's life.

In 1929, Jesse met Charles Riley. Mr. Riley was
a teacher and the track team coach at Fairmount
Junior High. He had seen Jesse running with
friends at lunchtime. He watched Jesse running
on the playground and saw something special. He
offered to help him become an even better runner.

Chapter 3
School Days

Jesse wanted to work with Coach Riley, but there was a big problem. Jesse had so many jobs after school, he had little time to train! Coach Riley agreed to meet him early in the morning before school started. He showed Jesse how to run smoothly and easily. He told Jesse to run as if he were stepping over hot coals, to stay strong and straight and light.

Coach Riley also welcomed Jesse into his home and invited him over for dinner. Jesse later said that Coach Riley was the first white person he had ever really known.

At age seventeen Jesse began taking classes at East Technical High School. By then, all his siblings were working full-time; none had finished high school. Jesse wanted to be different.

He saw attending high school and being on the track team as the pathways to success. Fortunately for him, Coach Riley had been asked to help with East Technical's track team.

Jesse's great speed and Riley's coaching were a winning combination. Jesse won race after race. He was best at sprinting, at the 100-yard and 220-yard dashes, which were the shortest races.

In 1932, Coach Riley introduced Jesse to gold-medal champion Charley Paddock, who had won the 100-meter dash (similar to the 100-yard dash) at the 1920 Olympics. Paddock also held the world 100-meter record at the time—10.4 seconds. He was known as the "fastest man in the world." Paddock talked to Jesse about how much hard work was required to be the best. Jesse was inspired by the great runner's words.

Even though he was still in high school, Jesse tried out for the 1932 Summer Olympics. Trials were held at Northwestern University in Evanston, Illinois, to find the best athletes for each race. Jesse had won a lot of high-school races but had never faced such skilled competitors before.

CHARLEY PADDOCK (1900–1943)

CHARLES PADDOCK WAS ONE OF THE BEST SPRINTERS OF THE EARLY TWENTIETH CENTURY. BORN IN TEXAS, HE WAS ONLY EIGHTEEN AND IN THE US ARMY WHEN HE WON HIS FIRST BIG RACES AT A MEET IN PARIS. THE FOLLOWING YEAR, HE WON THE 100-METER RACE AT THE 1920 OLYMPICS IN BELGIUM. HE EARNED A SECOND GOLD MEDAL IN THE 400-METER RELAY AND A SILVER FOR FINISHING SECOND IN THE 200-METER DASH. IN 1921, PADDOCK SET A WORLD RECORD BY RUNNING THE 100 METERS IN 10.4 SECONDS.

PADDOCK WAS FAMOUS FOR TAKING A BIG LEAP WITH HIS ARMS OUTSPREAD AS HE REACHED THE FINISH. HE SEEMED TO FLY OVER THE LINE. HE WAS A HANDSOME, WELL-SPOKEN MAN WHO ENJOYED ALL THE ATTENTION HIS FAMOUS SPEED BROUGHT HIM.

WHEN WORLD WAR II BEGAN, HE RETURNED TO THE MILITARY, SERVING IN THE MARINES. DURING THE WAR HE WAS KILLED IN AN AIRPLANE CRASH IN ALASKA.

Jesse ran well but didn't make the Olympic
team that year. Among the runners that beat
him was Eddie Tolan. At the 1932 Olympics,

Tolan became the first African American to win
the 100-meter gold medal.

Not long after the Olympics ended, Jesse
became a father. Ruth gave birth to their daughter
Gloria on August 8, 1932. Ruth still lived with
her parents, so they helped her raise the baby.

Jesse still lived with his parents, too. He helped
Ruth and the baby with money earned from his
after-school jobs.

All through the fall, Jesse's popularity grew.
His classmates chose him as president of the
student council. The track team made him captain.

By the spring of 1933, Jesse was setting records. In June of his senior year, he tied the world record in the 100-yard dash at just 9.4 seconds! His time of 20.7 seconds in the 220-yard race gave him a national high-school record, as did his long jump of 24 feet, 9 inches. All those records were set at a single high-school meet in Chicago. East Technical High scored a total of 54 points and won the meet. Jesse scored 30 points all by himself!

Newspapers from many US cities wrote articles about him and his records. Many track coaches hoped he would attend their universities.

The dream that Jesse had had on those long walks to church back in Alabama was coming true. He was going to college.

TRACK AND FIELD

TRACK AND FIELD WAS PART OF THE ANCIENT OLYMPIC GAMES IN GREECE NEARLY 2,800 YEARS AGO. IT IS ONE OF THE WORLD'S OLDEST ATHLETIC COMPETITIONS.

TODAY A TRACK-AND-FIELD COMPETITION IS USUALLY CALLED A *MEET*. TRACK EVENTS INCLUDE FOOTRACES OF MANY DIFFERENT DISTANCES, INCLUDING THE 100-METER, 200-METER, AND 400-METER DASHES AS WELL AS LONGER RACES SUCH AS RELAYS AND MARATHONS.

IN JESSE'S HIGH-SCHOOL AND COLLEGE MEETS, FOOTRACES WERE MEASURED IN YARDS. IN THE OLYMPICS AND OTHER INTERNATIONAL COMPETITIONS, THEY WERE MEASURED IN METERS.

SHORT RACES ARE CALLED *SPRINTS*, OR *DASHES*, WHILE LONGER ONES, SUCH AS THE 5,000- AND 10,000-METER EVENTS, ARE CALLED *DISTANCE* RACES. IN SPRINTS, EACH RUNNER RUNS THE ENTIRE RACE INSIDE HIS OR HER OWN LANE TO AVOID BUMPING INTO OTHER RUNNERS.

FIELD EVENTS INVOLVE JUMPING AND THROWING. THE AIM OF THE LONG JUMP, FOR EXAMPLE, IS TO SPRINT ALONG A RUNWAY AND LEAP AS FAR AS POSSIBLE, LANDING IN A PIT OF SAND. OTHER FIELD EVENTS INCLUDE THE HIGH JUMP, THE POLE

VAULT, THE JAVELIN THROW, THE SHOT PUT, AND
THE DISCUS THROW. RESULTS ARE GIVEN IN BOTH
FEET AND METERS.

SOME EVENTS COMBINE RUNNING AND JUMPING.
IN HURDLING, LOW WOODEN BARRIERS ARE SPACED
EQUALLY ALONG A TRACK. WHILE RUNNING FULL
SPEED, SPRINTERS MUST LEAP OVER EACH HURDLE
IN TURN.

Chapter 4
College Man

Jesse chose to attend Ohio State University in Columbus, about 145 miles from his home in Cleveland. Many of his Black fans were disappointed. They thought he should attend an all-Black university. And sportswriters for Black newspapers agreed. Throughout his life, Jesse tried to ignore such criticism. He wanted to live as he saw fit, regardless of his race; he didn't want race to separate people.

Life at Ohio State was not always easy. In 1934, out of more than fifteen thousand students, only about one hundred were Black. Though Ohio was not a Jim Crow state, the university was segregated. Jesse could not live on campus. When his track team traveled south, he and the other Black team members sometimes had to eat on the bus while their white teammates ate in a restaurant.

But he tried hard not to let such racism bother him. "If someone [said something racist] to him, Jesse would say, 'That's his problem, not mine,'" fellow runner Louis Zamperini later said.

As he had done in the past, Jesse worked while he went to school. He worked at a gas station, at the school library, and even at the Ohio Statehouse. While white students got to operate passenger elevators at the statehouse, Jesse had to operate a freight elevator in the back of the building.

On the track, Ohio State coach Larry Snyder
picked up where Charles Riley left off. Jesse felt
his coach respected him as a person, regardless

of his race. Coach Snyder took Jesse to local schools to meet children. And he asked Jesse to speak at lunches for businessmen and Ohio State supporters. Coach Snyder had been a track star at Ohio State himself. He introduced new training methods, including having team members work out in time to music played over stadium loudspeakers.

Ohio State was part of the Big Ten, an athletic organization of ten large midwestern schools. The 1934 Big Ten Conference track-and-field meet was a showcase for Jesse. He won the 100-yard dash, the 220-yard race, and the long jump.

Before his second season, Jesse was named captain of the Ohio State team. He was the first Black person to earn that honor for any sport in the Big Ten.

Chapter 5
An Amazing Day

At the end of the track season, the top athletes from each Big Ten school gathered for a championship meet. The 1935 Big Ten Championships were held at Ferry Field at the University of Michigan.

It was the biggest event of the track season for Ohio State. But Jesse nearly did not make it.

About a week before the big day, he was wrestling with some friends. He accidentally fell down some stairs and hurt his back. He was in great pain and thought he might not be able to compete. Coach Snyder did not want Jesse to run and put his future in danger, no matter how important the meet was to the school.

But Jesse worked with the team trainers all week to get better. He got massages. He took hot baths and did stretches and exercises.

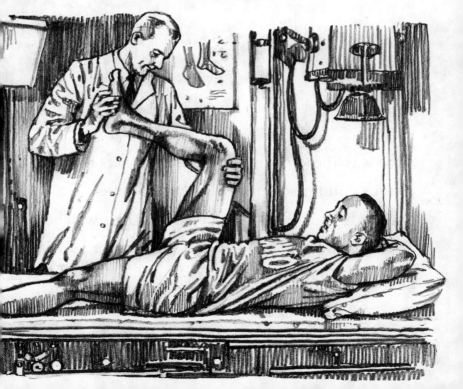

On May 25, 1935, he showed up at Ferry Field and made history.

At 3:15 p.m., aching back and all, Jesse lined up for the 100-yard dash. When the starting gun went off, he flew out of his starting crouch.

He was ahead of the rest of the runners in a few yards and burst through the finish tape a few seconds later. The timers checked their watches: 9.4 seconds! He had tied the world record set in 1930 by Frank Wykoff!

Fifteen minutes later, Jesse took his first long jump. He sprinted down the runway. He stepped hard on the takeoff board and leaped. When he landed, he had jumped farther than anyone in history—26 feet, 8¼ inches! His jump broke the old record by six inches—an accomplishment no one expected. In the long jump, a new record was usually set by an inch or two at a time.

Only nine minutes later, Jesse was at it again. This time the event was the 220-yard dash, straight down the track. Once again he pulled ahead of the other runners and finished far in the lead. His time of 20.3 seconds also set a world record!

After resting briefly and stretching his injured back, he returned to the track at 4:00 p.m. Just 22.6 seconds later, he won his fourth event, the 220-yard low hurdles. He had claimed his *third* world record of the day! In less than an hour, he had set or tied four world records. No one before or since has matched that feat.

When Jesse returned to his house that night, his back hurt so much that, he later said, "they had to carry me up the stairs."

Because of his amazing talents, Jesse was becoming known throughout the United States. Sports fans read about him in newspapers everywhere. When Ohio State finished second in the national championships, Jesse scored 40 of the team's 40.5 points. The *New York Times* wrote about his

accomplishments on the front page of the sports section. As he won race after race for Ohio State, people saw him in newsreels in movie theaters. Black people especially began to follow him as one of their heroes, right up there with champion boxer Joe Louis. They all wondered if he could keep running fast enough to win Olympic gold.

JOE LOUIS (1914–1981)

JOSEPH LOUIS BARROW, KNOWN AS JOE LOUIS, WAS AN AMERICAN PROFESSIONAL BOXER. NICKNAMED *THE BROWN BOMBER*, HE WAS THE FIRST AFRICAN AMERICAN TO ACHIEVE NATIONWIDE RECOGNITION AS A SPORTS HERO.

LOUIS HELD THE TITLE OF WORLD HEAVYWEIGHT CHAMPION FOR A RECORD TWELVE YEARS, FROM 1937 TO 1949. HE IS CONSIDERED ONE OF THE GREATEST HEAVYWEIGHT BOXERS OF ALL TIME.

Chapter 6
An Olympic Trip

In the summer of 1935, Jesse and Ruth finally married. He was still in school, while she was caring for baby Gloria. In the fall, when the school year began, Jesse struggled on the track for the first time, losing several key races. Up until now, he had kept his grades high enough to stay in school. But suddenly he was suspended from the track team due to bad grades. He knew the Olympics tryouts would be held that summer. He worked hard in class over the winter and was allowed to return to the team and prepare for the Games.

In July 1936, Jesse traveled to New York City for races that would decide who would represent the United States in that year's Summer Olympics. In New York, he won three events: the 100- and 200-meter dashes and the long jump. Another

dream had come true: He was an Olympian!
The Games would be held in Berlin, Germany,
in August.

As he prepared for the long trip, important
events were unfolding in Europe. Adolf Hitler had
become Germany's powerful leader. He was head
of the National Socialist German Workers' Party,
commonly known as the Nazis. Hitler and the
Nazis hated anyone who was not "fully German."

They hated Jews, handicapped people, gay and lesbian people, and Black people. They chased thousands of people out of the country, even those who had been German citizens their entire lives.

The news from Germany frightened many Americans. They believed participating in the 1936 Berlin Olympics would give power to Hitler, and many were disgusted by Nazi ideas. Many called for the United States to boycott.

Jesse didn't share Hitler's views, but he was against a boycott. Coach Snyder believed the Olympics were what Jesse had been waiting for. By going to Berlin and winning, Snyder told him, Jesse could show the world how great he was. He could also show Hitler what a Black athlete could accomplish.

HITLER AND THE NAZIS

IN 1933, THE NATIONAL SOCIALIST GERMAN WORKERS' PARTY CAME TO POWER IN GERMANY. COMMONLY KNOWN AS THE NAZIS, THEY BELIEVED THAT ONLY "PURE" GERMANS DESERVED TO LIVE IN THEIR COUNTRY. THEY PERSECUTED ANYONE THEY BELIEVED DID NOT BELONG, INCLUDING JEWS, CATHOLICS, ROMANI PEOPLE, GAY AND LESBIAN PEOPLE, AND BLACK PEOPLE. THEIR LEADER WAS ADOLF HITLER. HITLER EVENTUALLY DIRECTED HIS ARMY AND SECRET POLICE TO KILL AS MANY JEWISH PEOPLE AS POSSIBLE, A TRAGIC PLAN TODAY KNOWN AS THE HOLOCAUST.

IT WAS HITLER'S GOAL TO EXPAND GERMANY BY INVADING NEIGHBORING COUNTRIES. IN 1939, GERMANY ATTACKED NEARBY NATIONS IN EUROPE, AND WORLD WAR II BEGAN.

BY THE TIME GERMANY SURRENDERED IN 1945, HITLER HAD COMMITTED SUICIDE RATHER THAN FACE JUSTICE. THE HORRORS OF THE NAZI REGIME REMAIN ONE OF HISTORY'S DARKEST MOMENTS.

ADOLF HITLER

Important Black newspapers such as the *New York Amsterdam News* as well the National Association for the Advancement of Colored People (NAACP) urged Jesse and the other athletes to boycott. Some US senators and state governors felt the same way. And thousands of people attended rallies to call for a boycott.

Two groups had a say in the decision to send US athletes to the Games. The Amateur Athletic Union (AAU) spoke for track and field, the biggest and most important sport in the Olympics. The American Olympic Committee (AOC) was in charge of all US athletes, including the AAU group.

After months of debate, a vote was held by AAU leaders in December 1935. They voted 58.25 to 55.75 to send the team. It was a very close vote. Boycott supporters were shocked and feared the decision would give the impression that the United States supported the Nazis.

Once the decision was final, the American athletes, including Jesse, gathered to sail to Germany. A total of 359 American athletes—313 men and 46 women—would battle for gold medals in 19 sports.

Jesse joined the entire US Olympic team on a huge ship, the S.S. *Manhattan*. Dressed in blue blazers and wearing straw hats called boaters, the athletes waved from the deck as the United States slipped away behind them. For more than a week, the Americans lived together on the ship.

More Black athletes made up the track team
than ever before, and they mixed easily with the
white athletes, who recognized only skill, not skin
color. Photographers captured Jesse practicing his
hurdles on the deck of the ship. He jogged the
long, wide walkways to stay in shape.

BERLIN OLYMPIC STADIUM

The American athletes would join Olympians from forty-eight other countries. More than 4,400 men and women would compete in a wide range of sports, including track and field, rowing, gymnastics, weightlifting, fencing, and field hockey. The German team had 348 athletes, one of the largest groups entered.

In Germany, Jesse was greeted warmly as an athletic hero. His world records and performance on the track had already made him famous. The German government may have felt otherwise, but the German people wanted to see the great athlete in person.

Chapter 7
A Legend Is Born

On August 1, athletes from forty-nine nations marched into Olympic Stadium at the Opening Ceremonies. Bands played, pigeons were released in celebration, and the Olympic torch arrived in front of more than one hundred thousand spectators.

The Berlin Olympics marked the first time the torch was carried from city to city in the host country before arriving at the stadium. This tradition has been a part of the Olympics ever since.

On August 3, Jesse competed in the finals
for the 100-meter dash. He approached the
starting line. Next to him were runners from the
Netherlands, Germany, and Sweden, along with
two fellow Americans. He carefully dug his feet
into the small holes he had made in the track. The
imprints would help him start running quickly.

The crowd grew silent, awaiting the starting pistol. *Crack!* At the sound, Jesse and the other five runners sprinted forward. The race was close for only a moment. Then Jesse pulled ahead. Running with his usual calm, easy grace, he sprinted across the finish line first. He was a gold-medal champion . . . and now the "fastest man in the world."

Soon he stood atop a small platform called a podium. One step below him stood silver-medalist Ralph Metcalfe. Hitler and the Nazis believed white people were the greatest race on the planet. Jesse Owens and Ralph Metcalfe had proven them wrong. The bronze medalist was Martinus Osendarp from the Netherlands. Jesse was presented with a crown of laurel leaves, an Olympic tradition dating back to ancient Greece.

A gold medal was placed around his neck. He stood at attention as "The Star-Spangled Banner" was played in the heart of Nazi Germany.

"The competition was grand, and I'm glad to come out on top," Jesse told reporters.

As he walked off the field after the medal ceremony, he was led toward the stands. From his seat high above, Hitler was seen to give a short wave, a version of the Nazi salute. But Hitler did not personally greet the new Olympic champion.

Hitler *had* publicly congratulated two German athletes the day before. After that he did not congratulate athletes from any other nation.

By the next day, American newspapers were reporting that Hitler had "snubbed" Owens by not shaking his hand after the race. If true, it was a great insult, and many Americans reacted with anger. Newspaper headlines back in the US said that the German leader had refused to meet

the African American gold medalist. The *Baltimore Afro-American* wrote "Adolf Snubs US Lads." However, other reporters on the scene in Berlin did not report such news. The *Pittsburgh Courier* wrote "Germany officially explained that Hitler did not intend to slight our athletes."

Whether Hitler snubbed Jesse or not, it was well-known that Nazis believed Black people to be less than human. Hitler and his followers were extreme racists. "White humanity should be ashamed of itself" for letting Black athletes win, wrote Joseph Goebbels, a top Nazi official. Around the world, more and more people began to realize that it was the Nazis who should be ashamed.

Chapter 8
Golden Moments

Jesse's success at the Olympic Games continued. His next event was the long jump, held on August 4. His toughest rival was a jumper named Luz Long. Luz was German but did not share the views of Hitler and the Nazis. He respected Jesse as a fellow competitor. To reach the event finals, each athlete had to make a jump of at least 23 feet, 5½ inches. Jesse

LUZ LONG

had jumped that far in high school, so it should have been no problem. But Jesse made a foul on his first qualifying jump by stepping too far past the takeoff board. If Jesse fouled again, he would be out of the finals. Luz came over to Jesse and suggested that Jesse move his takeoff point back just to be safe. Jesse did, and on his next jump, he easily qualified for the final. After that jump, Jesse shook Luz's hand in thanks.

The long-jump final came down to just Jesse and Luz. Jump after jump, they topped each other.

Finally, Jesse jumped 26 feet. "I decided I wasn't going to come down. I was going to fly. I was going to stay up in the air forever," he said later.

Luz could not match that distance, and Jesse earned his second gold medal. Luz hugged Jesse after they got their medals and escorted him around the stadium, arm in arm, as the German fans cheered. Jesse said he would always remember Luz Long's great sportsmanship.

On August 5, Jesse competed for his third gold medal, this time in the 200-meter dash. By now, German fans understood they were watching a true champion. As the runners prepared for the event, the fans chanted Jesse's last name in their German accent: "Oh-vens! Oh-vens! Oh-vens!" With a time of 20.7 seconds, Jesse set a world record and won his third gold medal. After the medal ceremony, he happily signed autographs for his German fans.

American team leaders wanted Jesse to run again, this time in the 4 × 100-meter relay. In this race, four runners pass a baton from hand to hand as each finishes a 100-meter section. But four runners had already been assigned to this race. By swapping in Jesse and silver-medalist Ralph Metcalfe, the US committee hoped, it said, to secure another gold medal. To make room for Jesse and Metcalfe, the coaches removed two other runners, Marty Glickman and Sam Stoller.

SAM STOLLER AND MARTY GLICKMAN

This move was very surprising. Owens and Metcalfe did not become part of the relay team until the last minute. Many people, including Glickman and Stoller, thought there was another reason for the change. "If you drop us, there's going to be [a lot of controversy]," said Glickman. "We're the only two Jews on the track team."

Although no official reason was ever given, historians believe the US team changed runners

after a demand from the Nazis, who hated Jews even more than they hated Black people.

Jesse didn't want to do it. "I've got three medals. I don't need any more," he said. But US team leaders forced him to run.

Jesse, Metcalfe, Foy Draper, and Frank Wykoff raced to victory in the relay. Their time of 39.8 seconds set a world record. It was Jesse's fourth gold medal.

In a little less than a week, he had done something remarkable. He was the first American athlete ever to win four track-and-field gold medals at a single Olympics. Looking back to the beginning of his gold-medal winning streak, he often said, "It was the happiest day of my life."

Chapter 9
Life After the Olympics

After the games
were over, Jesse
sailed home to
America. He left
ahead of the US
team, which went
on a tour of other
European cities.
Jesse had chosen
not to join them.
In New York City
a huge crowd

welcomed him when he arrived. He was greeted
by his family members, too, who had traveled
from Cleveland for the occasion.

Even amid the celebration, there were signs of America's continuing racial divide. By 1920, New York was home to more Black people than any other northern city. The New York neighborhood known as Harlem—located in uptown Manhattan—was the center of Black American life. By 1936, Harlem boasted famous restaurants, churches, nightclubs, businesses, and newspapers, all owned and run by Black people. Downtown Manhattan was a different story.

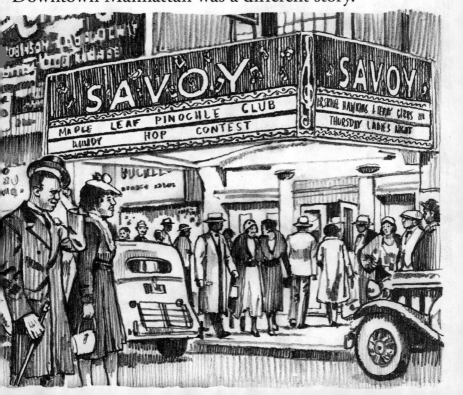

Jesse's parents, Henry and Emma, and his wife, Ruth, were refused service at several hotels downtown before they found one that would allow them to stay.

On his first night in New York, Jesse was taken to dinner at the Harlem home of Black entertainer Bill "Bojangles" Robinson. A dancer,

singer, and actor, Robinson was one of the most famous entertainers in the country. He was also one of few people to offer Jesse work after the Olympics. He invited him to appear in some of his shows and held a special dinner for him, where he introduced him to other entertainers. Robinson even asked his manager to help the star athlete.

THE HARLEM RENAISSANCE

BECAUSE OF THE GREAT MIGRATION, HARLEM HAD BECOME THE LARGEST BLACK NEIGHBORHOOD IN AMERICA. AFTER WORLD WAR I, IT ALSO BECAME THE SITE OF A MOVEMENT CALLED THE HARLEM RENAISSANCE. *RENAISSANCE* MEANS "REVIVAL" OR "REBIRTH." DURING THIS PERIOD, BLACK ARTISTS AND WRITERS IN HARLEM RENEWED THEIR CONNECTION TO THEIR HERITAGE.

POETS, NOVELISTS, AND WRITERS CREATED WORKS THAT CELEBRATED THE LIVES OF BLACK PEOPLE IN AMERICA. MAGAZINES SUCH AS *CRISIS* AND *OPPORTUNITY* GAVE EMERGING WRITERS SUCH AS LANGSTON HUGHES, COUNTEE CULLEN, AND ZORA NEALE HURSTON NEW PLACES TO SHARE THEIR WORK. PAINTERS CREATED ART THAT SHOWED THE STYLE AND ENERGY OF THE NEIGHBORHOOD. JAZZ AND THE BLUES, THE MUSIC OF BLACK PEOPLE IN AMERICA, GREW IN POPULARITY. AND ORGANIZATIONS SUCH AS THE NAACP HELPED ORGANIZE BLACK PEOPLE FIGHT FOR EQUAL RIGHTS.

THE HARLEM RENAISSANCE LASTED ONLY FROM 1918 TO 1937. BUT MANY BLACK WRITERS SINCE THEN WERE INSPIRED BY THOSE RENAISSANCE WRITERS. THE MUSIC OF THOSE TIMES HAS BECOME AN IMPORTANT PART OF AMERICAN LIFE. THE IDEAS OF EQUAL RIGHTS THAT STARTED IN THOSE DAYS GREW INTO THE CIVIL RIGHTS MOVEMENT OF THE 1960S. THE HARLEM RENAISSANCE MARKED THE BEGINNING OF AFRICAN AMERICAN CULTURAL EXPRESSION.

Then the Owens family returned to Cleveland for a celebration of his success. A huge crowd watched a parade through the city. Three days later, he was honored in the state capital of Columbus. The governor made a speech and gave Ruth a set of fancy silverware as a gift.

When the rest of the US Olympic team

returned from Europe three weeks later, Jesse
joined them in New York City for another parade.
Jesse again experienced the ups and downs of
his fame as a Black athlete. He rode in the front
car, but he sat with the famous pro boxer Jack
Dempsey, who had once said he would never fight
a Black man. Many Black people hated Dempsey.

They were uncomfortable that Jesse was sitting with
him. Also, many Black people were still upset with
Jesse for not boycotting the Games. As a result, he
was booed when the parade reached Harlem.

Also, reporters pointed out that the rest of the Black Olympic athletes were crowded together in a single car at the back of the long parade. Even in a city as great as New York, even in a strong Black community like Harlem, racism was still very evident.

By late summer 1936, after the parades and celebrations, Jesse faced new obstacles. While in Germany winning gold medals, he had received many job offers and opportunities for paid appearances back home. However, when he returned to America, nearly all the offers disappeared.

"It became increasingly [clear] that everyone was going to slap me on the back, want to shake my hand or have me up to their [hotel] suite," he said later. "But no one was going to offer me a job."

Only a few months after his Olympic triumph, he was offered a real, if strange, moneymaking opportunity. He was paid to fly to Cuba to race a horse called Julio McCaw. During halftime at a soccer game, Jesse easily outran the horse and took home $2,000, which was what most people made in an entire year.

"People said an Olympic champion [should not] race a horse," he said years later. "But you

can't eat four gold medals." Because he needed
to earn a living, he could not afford to take time
to finish his college degree. And since he had
become a professional athlete, he could not rejoin
the Ohio State track team.

Jesse was comfortable in front of people and
hoped his next career would involve performing
in some way. He went to work for Bojangles. After
taking some dancing lessons, he went on a short
tour with him.

Then, in early 1937, he got a job introducing and "leading" a twelve-piece band. It was a good job, but when the band's concerts were over, so was the job. He had to find other ways to make a living.

The next few years were a mix of joy and sadness. Jesse and Ruth had two more daughters, Marlene and Beverly. But in 1940, Henry Owens, Jesse's father, passed away.

Over the next decade, Jesse moved from job to job. White Olympians appeared in movies, or were paid to promote products. Black athletes like Jesse had few such opportunities. But as he said, he "hated to sit or to stand still."

In 1949, he moved his family to Chicago for a job with the Leo Rose Clothing Company, whose products he would help promote. He also worked with an insurance company and a Chicago hotel. Later, he was given a job with the Illinois State Athletic Commission. By the mid-1950s, things had improved quite a bit for him and his family. In 1950, the Associated Press had named him the greatest track athlete of the first half of the twentieth century.

The award slowly brought him back into the spotlight and reminded many fans of his great achievements. Jesse was soon being paid to give speeches all over the country and to act as a spokesman for a large oil company. His gold-medal success was finally paying off.

In 1955, President Dwight Eisenhower asked him to travel through Asia on behalf of the United States. Jesse visited Singapore, India, the Philippines, and Malaysia, among other nations. He was one of several well-known Americans sent abroad to promote democracy. "On our trip we are talking about our [American] way of life, the best way of life in the world," he said.

Chapter 10
A Legacy of Strength

Though he was traveling the world and speaking about how great life was in the United States, life was not great for many Black people,

especially in the South. America was still a racially divided country. To try to change that, many African Americans joined the Civil Rights Movement as the 1960s began. They rallied and marched, calling for an end to Jim Crow laws and other forms of racism. Some leaders in the movement wanted Jesse to support their cause through speeches. However, he chose not to.

At that time, he believed protest was not the

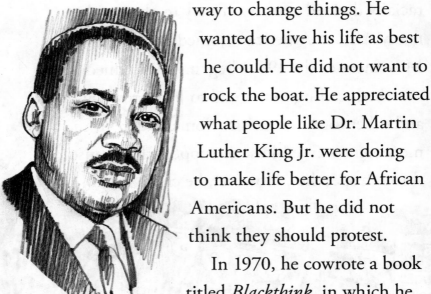

way to change things. He wanted to live his life as best he could. He did not want to rock the boat. He appreciated what people like Dr. Martin Luther King Jr. were doing to make life better for African Americans. But he did not think they should protest.

DR. MARTIN LUTHER KING JR.

In 1970, he cowrote a book titled *Blackthink,* in which he expressed these feelings. "If the Negro doesn't succeed in today's America," he wrote, "it is because he has chosen to fail." He wrote that he believed that arguing and protesting were not the answers to America's problems with race. Many of his longtime admirers were shocked and hurt.

They were angry that a Black hero like Jesse

had said he was not on their side. For the first time in his life, he received hate mail. Hearing from other Black people changed him. He realized he had been focusing on his own story and not appreciating the troubles other Black people endured. He finally understood what the Civil Rights Movement was all about.

Two years later, he wrote another book, *I Have Changed*. In it, he apologized for *Blackthink*. Finally, Jesse understood the goals of the Civil Rights Movement more clearly.

Throughout the 1960s and 1970s, Jesse was paid to appear in advertisements for products such as credit cards, cigars, and soup. He also ran an advertising business that helped companies make ads and get attention for their products. All of his and Ruth's

I HAVE CHANGED

A SHOCKINGLY PERSONAL STATEMENT IN A TRAGICALLY IMPERSONAL TIME

BY JESSE OWENS
WITH PAUL NEIMARK

three daughters graduated from college, including two who had attended Ohio State. In 1961, Marlene had become the first African American woman named homecoming queen at OSU.

In the early 1970s, Jesse and Ruth moved from Chicago to Arizona.

In the 1970s, Jesse again played a role in the Olympics. In 1972, he was honored at the Summer Olympics in Munich, Germany. He returned to the country where he first won Olympic glory. The organizers of the Games gave him a special award, and once again he heard cheers from a huge crowd. And in 1973, he was elected to the board of directors of the US Olympic Committee.

Over the next few years, he received many other awards. Ohio State gave him an honorary college degree. He had never graduated from the school, so the degree meant a great deal to him. The NCAA, which organizes college sports, gave him the 1974 Theodore Roosevelt Award. That same year, he was elected to the International Track and Field Hall of Fame.

The Presidential Medal of Freedom is the
highest honor the United States can bestow on
a citizen. President Gerald Ford gave this award
to Jesse in thanks for his support of his country
during his travels, and in honor of his athletic
success.

Though Jesse was still traveling and giving
speeches, he was also enjoying a quiet life with
Ruth in the warm weather of Arizona. But in 1979,

three years after receiving the Presidential Medal, he learned he had lung cancer. On March 31, 1980, he died of the disease at his home in Arizona. He was sixty-six years old.

Jesse's Olympic legacy continues. In 1984, his granddaughter Gina was chosen to carry the torch into Memorial Coliseum to start the Los Angeles Olympics.

Decades later, Jesse's amazing accomplishments on the track remain among the greatest in American sports history. His success in the face of Nazi hatred remains an inspiration. His life after the Olympics was not as glorious, but he faced it with the same strength and hard work that made him a champion.

THE 100–METER DASH
AFTER JESSE OWENS

JESSE OWENS'S BEST TIME IN THE 100-METER DASH WAS 10.2 SECONDS. HE HELD THE WORLD RECORD FOR TWENTY YEARS, UNTIL WILLIE WILLIAMS FINISHED THE RACE IN 10.1 SECONDS IN 1956.

THE WORLD RECORD AS OF 2015 IS 9.58
SECONDS, SET IN 2009 BY JAMAICA'S USAIN BOLT.
THAT MEANS THAT AFTER SEVENTY-EIGHT YEARS,
RUNNERS HAVE IMPROVED JESSE'S RECORD BY
ONLY A LITTLE MORE THAN A HALF SECOND!

TIMELINE OF JESSE OWENS'S LIFE

1913	Jesse Owens is born in Oakville, Alabama
1921	Moves with family to Cleveland, Ohio
1932	Daughter Gloria born
1933	Begins studying at Ohio State University
1935	At Big Ten Championships, sets three world records and ties another in less than an hour Marries Ruth Solomon
1936	Wins four gold medals at Summer Olympics in Berlin, Germany
1939	Daughter Marlene born
1940	Daughter Beverly born
1949	Moves with family to Chicago
1950	Is named top track athlete of the first half of the twentieth century
1955	Sent on international goodwill tour by President Eisenhower
1960	Starts his own advertising and marketing company
c. 1971	Moves with Ruth to Arizona
1973	Elected to board of directors of US Olympic Committee
1976	Given Presidential Medal of Freedom
1980	Dies of lung cancer in Arizona at age sixty-six

TIMELINE OF THE WORLD

United States introduces income tax	1913
The first Winter Olympic Games held in France	1924
Charles Lindbergh is the first person to fly solo across the Atlantic Ocean	1927
Adolf Hitler elected chancellor of Germany	1933
Germany invades Poland, starting World War II	1939
Japan bombs Pearl Harbor, driving US to enter World War II	1941
US drops two atomic bombs on Japan World War II ends	1945
Korean War begins	1950
Brown vs. Board of Education ruling by Supreme Court ends school segregation	1954
March on Washington and major civil rights rally President John F. Kennedy is assassinated	1963
Civil Rights Act passed by Congress, making all segregation illegal	1964
Civil rights leader Martin Luther King Jr. assassinated	1968
Palestinian terrorists kill eleven Israeli athletes and coaches at the Summer Olympics in Munich, Germany	1972
Last US forces leave Vietnam at the end of Vietnam War	1975
America celebrates the Bicentennial, its two hundredth birthday	1976
To protest the Soviet invasion of Afghanistan, the US does not send athletes to the Summer Olympics in Moscow	1980

BIBLIOGRAPHY

Baker, William J. **Jesse Owens: An American Life**. New York: The Free Press, 1986.

* Edmondson, Jacqueline. **Jesse Owens: A Biography**. Westport, CT: Greenwood Press, 2007.

* Gigliotti, Jim. **Jesse Owens: Gold Medal Hero**. New York: Sterling Publishing, 2010.

* McKissack, Patricia and Fredrick. **Jesse Owens: Olympic Star**. Berkeley Heights, NJ: Enslow Publishers, 2001.

Schaap, Jeremy. **Triumph: The Untold Story of Jesse Owens and Hitler's Olympics**. Boston: Houghton Mifflin, 2007.

* Books for young readers